W9-BTM-615

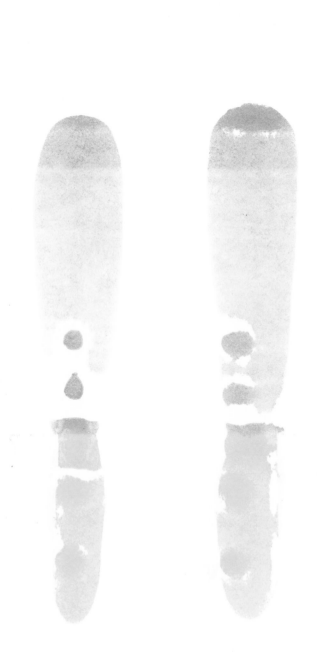

Music Matters

CLASSICAL
MUSIC

Clive D. Griffin

Dryad Press Limited   London

Typeset by Tek-Art Ltd, Kent
and printed and bound by
Richard Clay Ltd
Chichester, Sussex
for the Publishers,
Dryad Press Limited,
8 Cavendish Square,
London W1M 0AJ

ISBN 0 8521 9756 X

ACKNOWLEDGMENTS

The Author and Publishers thank the following
for their kind permission to reproduce
copyright illustrations: BBC Hulton Picture
Library, pages 6, 8, 11, 13, 15, 16, 22, 23, 25,
26, 27, 30, 33, 34, 36, 38, 39, 40, 41, 42, 51, 52,
54; Peter Bloomfield, page 57; Imperial War
Museum, pages 44, 45; John Price Studios,
London, page 49 (bottom); The Photo Source,
frontispiece, pages 10, 18, 28, 29, 31, 32, 46,
49 (top), 56. The maps on pages 21 and 62 are
by R.F. Brien.
    The cover photograph shows the BBC
Symphony Orchestra, conducted by Sir John
Pritchard, in a rehearsal for the "First Night of
the Proms" 1987 (Photo: Alex von Koettlitz).

CONTENTS

INTRODUCTION

Like "jazz", the term "classical music" is a convenient label to describe a variety of styles. It cover the works of composers as different as Bach and Schoenberg, ranging from baroque to serialism. It should not be confused with Classical music (with a capital C) which refers to the music of the late eighteenth century.

Composers should not be regarded as people living in isolation from everyday life. They need to make a living just like the rest of us and are influenced by contemporary political and social events. The aim of this book is to look at some of the ways in which they have been affected by their historical surroundings, and the impact of their own personalities and beliefs upon their music. For this reason, the book follows a thematic rather than a strictly chronological approach and avoids detailed musical analysis. For convenience, however, it is divided into three sections which correspond roughly with the eighteenth, nineteenth and twentieth centuries. Historical background information has been given where necessary and, whenever possible, composers have been allowed to speak for themselves.

PART ONE

EARNING A LIVING

The idea of the composer as an artist is a relatively recent one. In the eighteenth century, composers were seen as skilled craftsmen, supplying music for particular occasions or patrons. They did not write with the intention that their music would live on after them. Indeed, many were not even particularly noted as composers in their own time. J.S. BACH, for example, was better known as an organist and an organ technician. It was possible to earn a living from writing music, but composers needed either employment from the Church or in royal courts, or the support of rich patrons.

The Church

The religious wars which had ravaged Europe since the Reformation had come to an end by the eighteenth century but their after-effects remained. The religious differences between the Roman Catholic and Protestant Churches were also reflected in musical differences. The Society of Jesus, founded by Saint Ignatius Loyola in 1540, used many means to draw people back to the Catholic Church. One of these was the encouragement of new styles of religious music. The essence of such music was contrast – contrast between solo singers and choirs, between instrumentalists and singers and in volume and mood. Such ideas were viewed with a certain amount of suspicion in Protestant lands, where a much stricter attitude towards the function of music in church prevailed. The English evangelist, John Wesley, for example, frowned upon contrapuntal music because different words were often sung at the same time. To such people, the clear transmission of religious texts was far more

important than musical effects, however beautiful they might be. New ideas did find their way into Protestant music, but they were not always welcomed at first. The twenty-one-year-old Bach was rebuked, when organist at Arnstadt, "for having hitherto made many curious variations in the chorale, and mingled many strange tones in it, and for the fact that the congregation has been confused by it".

JOHANN SEBASTIAN BACH (1685-1750) was the greatest of all composers of religious music in the Protestant tradition, but he was not recognized as such during his own lifetime. When he obtained a post at Leipzig, he was the third-choice candidate. "Since the best man could not be obtained, mediocre ones would have to be accepted," was the comment of his new employers! Johann Sebastian was a member of a large musical family – there were Bachs working as musicians all over Germany, in Arnstadt, Hamburg, Berlin, Dresden, Weimar and Leipzig. His father, Johann Ambrosius, was church organist at Eisenach. Johann Sebastian's life was spent in a series of positions as organist and teacher at the chapels of various German courts or in the service of the Church.

John Wesley (1703-91) *English preacher and founder of the Methodist Church.*

---

contrapuntal: *counterpoint is the simultaneous combination of two or more melodies. Contrapuntal is the adjective used to describe such music.*

---

chorale: *a type of slow and stately German hymn tune.*

J.S. Bach was a deeply religious man, and a devout Lutheran, but it should not be assumed that his life was one of blameless saintliness. He was constantly quarrelling with his employers – over money, the music he composed, his precise duties, and the behaviour of students under his charge. In 1706, he was in trouble for staying away from his duties (he was given four weeks' leave which he extended to sixteen). He was reproved for playing for too long on the organ during services. (He answered by going to the opposite extreme and hardly playing at all.) He was attacked for being too critical – in at least one case, physically attacked: in 1705, a student called Geyersbach, angry at having his bassoon playing compared to the bleating of a nanny goat, assaulted Bach in the street. Swords were drawn but no permanent injury was done. At Weimar, he annoyed his employer, the Grand Duke, so much that he was actually imprisoned for a short time.

The last twenty years of his life were spent at Leipzig, where he was cantor of St Thomas's School. (The cantor was in charge of the choir.) Bach was a member of the teaching staff and his subjects included Latin and singing. He was also responsible for the music – its composition and performance – in all four of the city's churches. (It must be remembered that at this time education was almost entirely in the hands of the Church.) By all accounts, St Thomas's School was not the kind of place one would have been proud to be associated with. The buildings were old and neglected – "a hotbed of disease". The students of the school were wild and undisciplined and the staff were no better. The latter were constantly quarrelling amongst themselves and neglecting their duties. The inhabitants of the town thought poorly of the school and sent their children elsewhere if possible.

The school provided choirs for the local churches, money having been bequeathed to them for this purpose. Boys were selected for the school after

JOHANN SEBASTIAN BACH, from a painting by L. Sichling.

examination. Bach constantly complained about having to make do with inadequate resources. In 1730, he outlined his ideal musical requirements as a choir of twelve to sixteen singers and an orchestra of eighteen to twenty players. What he actually had was eight musicians and singers whom he summed up as follows: seventeen "unusable", twenty "not yet usable" and seventeen "unfit". With these resources, he was required to provide weekly cantatas for the city's churches as

---

cantata: *a musical setting of a text, generally religious, consisting of sections for both solo voices and full choir.*

6

well as special music for Christmas, Easter and Whitsun. He could also make money "on the side" by producing music for weddings and funerals. As he said himself, "When there are rather more funerals than usual, the fees rise in proportion; but when a healthy wind blows, they fall accordingly."

Bach did what he could with the limited forces at his disposal. His son, Carl Philipp Emanuel, noted that he was particularly fussy about tuning. "Nobody could tune his instruments to please him. He did everything himself . . . he heard the slightest wrong note even in the largest ensembles." The rector (head) of St Thomas's School described how Bach conducted a performance, not only playing his own part but making sure everyone else came in at the right time,

"the one with a nod, another by tapping with his feet, the third with a warning finger, giving the right note to one from the top of his voice, to another from the bottom, and a third from the middle of it – all alone, in the midst of the greatest din made by all the participants, and, although he is executing the most difficult parts himself, noticing at once whenever and wherever a mistake occurs, holding everybody together, taking precautions everywhere and repairing any unsteadiness, full of rhythm in every part of his body."
(Harold Schonberg, *The Lives Of The Great Composers*, Davis-Poynter Ltd, 1970)

When Bach took over as cantor at Leipzig, he dispensed with all the music his predecessor had produced, and he fully expected that his successor would do the same. Music at that time was more concerned with what was *being* made rather than what *had* been made. Bach's music was kept alive, however. His successor at Leipzig continued to perform it at services and it was known to many

professional musicians. Four of his sons went on to become noted composers in their own right. His wife, Anna Magdalena, however, ended her days in an almshouse and was buried in a pauper's grave.

Court musicians

The period of European history from the end of the Thirty Years War (1648) to the French Revolution (1789) is referred to by historians as the *ancien régime*. Aristocratic government was almost universal and in parts of eastern Europe serfdom still existed. This was the time when many of the great royal houses were built or lavishly extended: Versailles in France, Het Loo in Holland, Kensington Palace and Hampton Court in England. Although we talk about England, France and Holland, the idea of the nation state as we know it was only just emerging. The monarchs of the *ancien régime* ruled collections of territories and provinces which were added to by marriage treaties or military conquest.

The map of Europe in the eighteenth century was very different from the one with which we are familiar today (see page 21). Many of the countries of modern Europe did not exist at all. What is now Germany, for example, was a collection of small states, each with its own royal household. In order to gain prestige, all of these states lavished money on the arts. The most famous centres of music were Potsdam, near Berlin, in Prussia; Dresden and Leipzig in Saxony; and Mannheim, the home of the Elector Palatine. The Mannheim orchestra was famous throughout Europe. It was very large for that time, consisting of some fifty players, described by one admirer as "an army of generals". The precision and power of the orchestra were of a standard previously unknown.

To the south of these German states was Austria, centre of the Hapsburg Empire whose lands included much of Eastern Europe as well as parts of Italy and Belgium. Austria had resisted the last

great Islamic campaign against Europe when a Turkish army was pushed back from the gates of Vienna in 1683. Following this, Vienna developed into one of the great cities of Europe, with grand palaces and churches, many built by Italian artists and craftsmen, and beautiful gardens. Vienna was a cosmopolitan city and became the major artistic capital of Europe.

It was here that FRANZ JOSEPH HAYDN was born in 1732. His childhood was an unhappy one, "more floggings than food" as he described it. At the age of eight he became a member of the choir of St Stephen's Cathedral in Vienna. Nine years later, his voice broke and he was dismissed. (There is also a story that his dismissal was partly provoked by an incident in which he cut off another choirboy's pigtail.) At the age of seventeen, he was left to make his own way in the world and for several years he all but starved. He eked out "a wretched existence" playing at social gatherings,

teaching and arranging music. He was by his own admission "a wizard on no instrument", but gradually his reputation improved. Eventually, in 1758, he gained a post as composer and music director for Count Ferdinand Maximilian von Morzin. Three years later, he entered the service of the Esterházy family, where he was to remain for the rest of his life.

Islamic invasions: *the Prophet Mohammed (570-632) claimed Allah's authority for spreading Islam by force. This Holy War (or jihad) took Muslim armies across north Africa and into north-west India. They swept into Spain in 711 and were finally checked at Poitiers in France in 732. From about 1000 until the end of the fifteenth century, the Turks spread Islam through Asia and into eastern Europe. The decline of the Turkish Empire ("The sick man of Europe") was the cause of several nineteenth-century wars as European countries tried to extend their influence at Turkey's expense.*

Prince Paul Anton Esterházy was a member of the wealthiest family in Hungary. Although Hungary was part of the Hapsburg Empire, the country's aristocratic families had considerable independence. Laws passed by the Empress Maria Theresa to improve the working conditions of the peasantry, for example, were ignored by wealthy Magyars. "God himself has differentiated between us," wrote one, "assigning to the peasant labour and need, to the lord, abundance and a merry life." A French traveller commented upon "the grinding poverty which in Hungary makes such nauseating contrast with the prodigality of the great" (E.N. Williams, *The Ancien Régime in Europe*, Bodley Head, 1970).

The written instructions relating to Haydn's appointment have been preserved and the following extracts give some idea of the duties and social standing of a court musician:

"His Highness expects Mr Haydn to behave as an honourable officer of a princely establishment. To wit: to be always sober, to behave not rudely but politely and with consideration towards the musicians under his direction, and to be modest, quiet and honest in his conduct. Whenever there is music for His Highness, Mr Haydn will be responsible not only for his own but for his musicians' becoming appearance in proper livery, according to instructions, with white stockings, white linen, well powdered, and either with pigtails or with hair-bags, but all in the same attire. . .

Mr Haydn will write at the order of his Highness such music as may be commanded. . .

Mr Haydn will appear every day, both in the morning and the afternoon, in the antechamber, to receive his orders for the day regarding the music. And having done so, he will communicate them to his musicians and make sure that they arrive punctually according to order. . .

It is his duty to take care of all the instruments with the utmost conscientiousness."

Other instructions required Haydn to "avoid undue familiarity in eating and drinking", to settle quarrels between musicians and to fine those who were unpunctual. Prince Paul died only a year after Haydn entered his service. He was succeeded by Prince Nicholas, a great lover of music. The prince played the baryton, a bass stringed instrument which had between 16 and 40 auxiliary wire strings running under the neck. These vibrated sympathetically with the six main strings. Developed during the late seventeenth century, the instrument, a very difficult one to play, was obsolete by the beginning of the nineteenth century. Prince Nicholas obviously thought that too little music had been written for the baryton. "Mr Haydn is reminded to apply himself more assiduously to composition than he has done so far, especially with regard to pieces for the gamba [the baryton], of which we have seen very little up to now; and, to show his zeal, he will hand in the first piece of every composition in a clean, tidy copy." Haydn obliged by producing 175 compositions for this obscure instrument.

Prince Nicholas, known as Nicholas the Magnificent, had a new palace built for himself. Its lavishness was matched only by that of the French royal palace at Versailles. Haydn does not seem to have been over-impressed, however, and preferred the prince's lengthy visits to Vienna to life in the Hungarian countryside. Upon returning from one such stay in the capital, he wrote the following letter to Frau Von Genzinger:

The palace of PRINCE ESTERHÁZY.

"Now – here I sit in my wilderness – deserted – like a poor orphan – almost without human company – sad – full of the memory of precious days gone by – yes, alas, gone by – and who knows when those pleasant days will return again? that charming company? . . . all those fine musical evenings. . . At home I found everything in confusion . . . nothing could comfort me . . . I got little sleep, even my dreams were a persecution, for when I dreamt that I was hearing an excellent performance of 'Le nozze di Figaro' that odious North wind woke me and almost blew my nightcap off my head. In three days I lost twenty pounds in weight, for the good Viennese titbits had already disappeared during the journey. Yes, yes, thought I to myself as I sat in my boarding house, obliged to eat a piece off a fifty-year-old cow instead of that delicious beef, an ancient mutton stew with yellow turnips instead of the ragout with little dumplings, a slice of roast leather instead of the Bohemian pheasant. . . Yes, yes, thought I to myself, if only I had here all those titbits I could not manage to eat at Vienna! – Here at Esterház nobody asks me – do you take chocolate with milk or without, would you like coffee, black or with cream, what can I get you, my dear Haydn, would you like vanilla ice or a pineapple one? If only I had here a piece of good Parmesan cheese, especially on fast days to help the black dumplings and noodles down more easily. . ."

(Quoted in Hans Gal (ed), *The Musician's World – Letters of the Great Composers*, Thames and Hudson, 1965)

Le nozze di Figaro: *Mozart's opera* The Marriage of Figaro.

FRANZ JOSEPH HAYDN composing at the keyboard. (From a painting by Gutenbrunner.)

In fact, Haydn led a very pleasant life at Esterház. He earned a good salary and had his own maid and coachman. Prince Nicholas established an orchestra of 20-25 players, not as large as the famous Mannheim orchestra but still a very respectable size and one of the best in Europe. Haydn was popular with the musicians under his charge and they referred to him affectionately as "papa". On one occasion, when the court musicians were growing restless and wished to visit their homes in Vienna, Hadyn obliged by writing a symphony in which the number of instruments playing the music of the last movement is gradually reduced, so that it ends with only one pair of violins on the platform. As each musician left the stage he blew out the candle on his music stand. This musical hint earned the symphony the nickname "The Farewell".

In 1790, Nicholas died. His successor, Prince Anton, disbanded the orchestra but retained the services of Haydn. He allowed him great freedom of movement, however, and Haydn spent much time in Vienna as well as travelling twice to London (in 1791-92 and 1794-95) where he enjoyed considerable success and financial reward. It should be remembered that travelling such distances in those days was no light matter. Even a Channel crossing was a perilous adventure. Haydn wrote about it in another of his letters to Frau Von Genzinger:

"... I hope, gracious madam, that you will have received my last letter from Calais. I ought to have sent a report as soon as I reached London, as I had promised, only I desired to wait for a few days that I might write of several matters together. I therefore report that on the first of the month, viz, New Year's Day, at half-past seven in the morning, after attending Mass, I went on board ship and, thanks be to the Almighty, reached Dover safe and sound at five o'clock in the afternoon. . .

During the entire crossing I remained on deck, in order to sate my eyes with that monstrous animal, the sea. So long as there was no wind, I was not afraid, but finally, as the wind grew ever stronger and I saw the high unruly waves breaking against the ship, I felt a little alarm, and with it a little nausea. However, I overcame it all and came safely into the harbour without vomiting. Most people were sick, and looked like ghosts. I took two days to recover."

Haydn enjoyed his time in London and wrote much about it in his diary. The entries include an account of a day at the Ascot races, one of the earliest descriptions of horse racing:

"The riders are very lightly clad in silk and each one has a different colour, so that you may recognize him more easily; no boots, a little cap on his head, they are all as lean as a greyhound and as lean as their horses. Everyone is weighed in, and a certain weight is allowed him, in relation to the strength of the horse, and if the rider is too light he must put on heavier clothes, or they hang some lead on him. . . . Among other things a single large stall is erected, wherein the Englishmen place their bets. The King has his own stall at one side. . . . Besides this, there are all sorts of other things – puppet plays, hawkers, horror plays – which go on during the races; many tents with refreshments, all kinds of wine and beer."
(Harold Schonberg, *The Lives Of The Great Composers*)

In 1795, Haydn returned to Esterház, where Nicholas II, Prince Anton's successor, had restored the orchestra. He wanted it mainly for use in church services and it was during this period that Haydn composed his greatest masses and the two oratorios, *The Creation* and *The Seasons*. It was also during this period that

Travel in the eighteenth century was no easy matter. The journey from London to York, for example, which can now be completed in a matter of hours, took four days. In bad weather, roads often became impassable and there are stories of coach passengers dying of exposure. The picture shows a coach leaving the Bell Savage Inn in London. Such coaching inns were a vital feature of eighteenth-century travel.

YORK Four Days Stage-Coach.

Begins on Friday the 12th of April. 1706.

ALL that are defirous to pafs from *London* to *York*, or from *York* to *London*, or any other Place on that Road; Let them Repair to the *Black Swan* in *Holbourn* in London, and to the *Black Swan* in *Coney* ftreet in *York*.

At both which Places, they may be received in a Stage Coach every *Monday, Wednefday* and *Friday*, which performs the whole Journey in Four Days, (if *God permits*,) And fets forth at Five in the Morning.

And returns from *York* to *Stamford* in two days, and from *Stamford* by *Huntington* to London in two days more. And the like Stages on their return.

Allowing each Paffenger 14l. weight, and all above 3d a Pound.

Performed By { Benjamin Kingman, Henry Harrifon, Walter Bayne's.

Alfo this gives Notice that Newcaftle Stage Coach, fets out from York, every Monday, and Friday, and from Newcaftle every Monday and Friday.

Rocth. in pt. of co. of Mr. Bod ingfel fer 5 p for Hunt ey the 3 of June 1706.

he composed the Austrian National Anthem. In 1802, he was released from his duties and settled in Vienna. He died there on 31 May 1809, the same day that Napoleon's troops entered the city. A day or two earlier, Hadyn had asked to be carried to the piano, where he played his National Anthem through three times as the thunder of the French guns bombarding Vienna sounded outside.

Rich patrons

Although travelling was no easy matter in the eighteenth century, there were some musicians who managed to establish themselves as an equivalent of the "international jet-setter". The more they established such reputations, the more they could rely upon the patronage of wealthy people who wished to be fashionable. This was particularly true in countries such as England where the absolute power of the monarchy had been broken and there was an emerging middle class, anxious to display its culture and breeding. The supreme musician in this arena, the first of the great musical impresarios, was GEORGE FRIDERIC HANDEL (1685-1759).

Born in Halle in what is now West Germany, Handel started his career as a church organist. He was attracted to the theatre, however, and in 1703 he moved to Hamburg, then a famous opera centre. Here he made friends with another German composer, Johann Mattheson, and he was employed to play the harpsichord for one of Mattheson's operas, *Cleopatra*. The harpsichord player's job was also to lead the orchestra. Mattheson was singing one of the leading parts but this was not enough for him and during the performance he came down into the orchestra and tried to take over at the harpsichord. Handel objected and swords were drawn, Mattheson's breaking on one of Handel's brass buttons as he lunged at him.

Handel did not confine himself to duelling with swords. There are also accounts of musical duels, including one on the harpsichord and organ with the Italian composer DOMENICO SCARLATTI. (Such musical duels were a feature of the eighteenth and early nineteenth centuries. Mozart and Clementi fought to a draw with the King of Prussia as umpire, while Beethoven had the reputation of being unbeaten.)

In 1710 Handel took up a position as court musician to the Elector of Hanover. Later the same year, he was granted permission to visit England and this was a tremendous success. He returned in 1712 and although it was supposed to be only for a temporary stay, he found London

The painter William Hogarth (1697-1764) ▶ *produced a series of engravings satirizing the manners and vices of eighteenth-century England. This illustration is from a series called* The Rake's Progress. *(A rake was a loose-living young man. The word was short for "rake-hell".) Hogarth's engravings show his progress through fashionable London society – a journey which leads eventually to the gallows. Here the rake is in the company of artists and musicians. The figure at the keyboard is a caricature of Handel.*

hard to resist. In the London of Alexander Pope and Jonathan Swift, of wits and gossips, scandals and scientific discoveries, Handel was recognized by all, according to Viscount Percival, as a "man of the vastest genius and skill in music that perhaps has lived since Orpheus". It is hardly surprising that he overstayed the period of his release from duties in Hanover. In 1714, however, Queen Anne of England, who had given Handel a pension of £200 a year, died childless. Her successor was George, Elector of Hanover, the employer from whom Handel had been absent for over two years. Legend has it that Handel composed his *Water Music* suite as a peace offering to the new King George I. The suite was certainly performed as accompaniment to a royal boat trip up the Thames and the King liked it so much "that he caused it to be played over three times in going and returning", but it seems that Handel had already made his peace with his employer.

impresario: *a producer or sponsor of public entertainment. A concert promoter.*

Hanover: *In 1714, Queen Anne of England was succeeded by her second cousin George, Elector (ruler) of Hanover. From 1714 to 1814, the Kings of England were also Electors of Hanover.*

He was granted a £400-a-year pension by George I and a further £200 from the Princess of Wales. Using this money, in addition to financial backing from members of the English nobility, Handel launched his own opera company. His operas, all performed in Italian according to the fashion of the day, were produced remarkably quickly. (Handel was a very fast composer, but he was also not above stealing ideas from other musicians or re-working music of his own.) Operas in Handel's day were very different from what one would expect nowadays: there was very little action and no attempt at creating convincing characters. They were mainly vehicles for singers, particularly the castratos, to show off their skills.

As their name implies, castratos were male singers who had been castrated in order to prevent their voices from breaking. They were selected as young boy singers, either orphans or from poor families who hoped for later financial reward. Although the operation, performed on boys between the ages of four and seven, was illegal, more than 4,000 boys were castrated in Italy during the eighteenth century. By 1640 castratos were used in church choirs throughout Italy and were beginning to appear in opera. Although originally given female roles, castratos were increasingly used for leading male characters. They retained youthful voices into old age but they suffered physically. Most were fat, with huge chests (and often female breasts) but thin arms and legs. The main claim to fame of castratos was their incredible breath control and their ability to execute complicated passages without any obvious strain. (The last castrato was Alessandro Moreschi who died in 1922. His voice was actually captured on a few

◄ *HANDEL's popularity in England is illustrated by this contemporary painting which shows the composer ascending to Heaven.*

early gramophone records.) Castratos were highly thought of, and were the first popular musical idols. They were pampered and over-indulged.

The ability to perform long, elaborate and highly ornamented vocal parts without any obvious signs of strain was also looked for in women singers. (*Coloratura* is the technical term for this style of singing.) The two most famous in Handel's day were Faustina Bordoni and Francesca Cuzzoni. These two hated each other and on one celebrated occasion started fighting on stage with much pulling of hair and scratching of faces, spurred on by their supporters in the audience. Audience behaviour at this time was rather different from today. There was no question of sitting quietly and listening. During performances audiences would chat, play cards, eat, heckle singers they didn't like and cheer those they did. Particular members of the nobility would have their own favourites and those who wished to ingratiate themselves with the nobility would follow suit. (Lord Burlington's followers supported Faustina Bordoni, for example, while Lady Pembroke's faction favoured Francesca Cuzzoni.) The opera was a social occasion, somewhere to be seen. The performers adopted a similar form of behaviour. When not actually singing, they would talk amongst themselves and greet friends in the audience.

Handel was not one to put up with the tantrums of singers. On one occasion when Francesca Cuzzoni refused to sing a particular aria, Handel grabbed hold of her and pushed her forward till she hung out of the window. Threatening to let go, he shouted, "Madame, I know you are a true she-devil, but I will show you that I am Beelzebub, the chief devil."

In the 1720s this style of opera went out of fashion, killed off by the success of John Gay's *Beggar's Opera*, a satirical work sung in English. Handel's company went bankrupt, but he had done so well during his time in London that he was able to put £10,000 into a new company. The new venture folded in 1737 and this time Handel lost a lot of money. He turned instead to the composition and production of oratorios. An oratorio is a dramatic work for voices and instruments, based on a religious theme, but it is not acted. The role of the chorus (choir) is much more important than in opera. Handel found a ready audience for his oratorios and composed almost twenty in less than fourteen years. These included his most enduring work, the *Messiah*, written in 1741. Handel appeared as organ soloist at every one of his oratorio presentations. He was still a popular musical figure and his blindness, which had become total by 1751, gained him extra sympathy.

He died in 1759 and was buried in Westminster Abbey, as a naturalized British subject. An obituary in the *Public Advertiser* contained the following acrostic:

> "He's gone, the Soul of Harmony is fled!
> And warbling Angels hover round him
> dead.
> Never, no, never since the Tide of Time
> Did music know a Genius so sublime!
> Each mighty harmonist that's gone
> before,
> Lessen'd to Mites when we his
> Works explore."

Although widely acknowledged as a genius in his own lifetime, and as the greatest composer of his day, WOLFGANG AMADEUS MOZART was one musician who did not manage to make a decent living in one of the ways outlined above. When he died in 1791, aged only thirty-five, he was buried in an unmarked common grave.

Born in Salzburg in 1756, Mozart was a child prodigy. At the age of three he could pick out tunes on the clavier; by four he

The MOZART family in about 1764. The young Wolfgang is seated at the keyboard while his father, Leopold, plays the violin and his sister, Maria Anna, sings.

could learn a piece of music in about half an hour and by the time he was six he was writing his own compositions. His older sister, Maria Anna, was also talented and the children's father, Leopold Mozart, was quick to exploit this. He took them "on the road", giving performances in the royal courts of Europe. The young Mozart was not only required to play; he also performed musical "tricks" such as playing the clavier with a cloth covering the keys. Leopold wanted to make sure that his son gained a good court position, but the unnatural life that he led retarded Mozart's normal growth to adulthood. As one of his earliest biographers said of him, "he never learned to rule himself. For domestic order, for sensible management of money, for moderation and wise choice in pleasures, he had no feeling."

Leopold secured a post for his son in the Archbishop's court at Salzburg, where he was employed himself. The younger Mozart hated everything about the court, however. He tried to gain employment elsewhere and was almost accepted by the Archduke Ferdinand of Austria. Unfortunately, the Archduke's mother, the Empress Maria Theresa, held the purse strings and objected to the appointment, "not believing that you need a composer or any useless people". Leopold allowed his son to travel throughout Europe in search of influential patrons, but he was to be disappointed; travelling only made the return to the court at Salzburg all the more depressing. Relations between Mozart and his employer grew steadily worse. In 1781, the Archbishop took his entire court retinue on a state visit to Vienna. In April, Mozart wrote the following letter to his father:

"...I told you in a recent letter that the Archbishop is a great hindrance to me here, for through him I have lost at least 100 ducats that I could certainly make by a concert in the theatre. ... Now that the public has come to know me, how much do you think I could earn if I gave a concert for my own benefit? But our Archbooby will not allow it."

Mozart was not prepared to submit to the restrictions imposed upon a court musician. He tried to resign his post, but the Archbishop would not see him. Eventually, in May 1781, he was literally kicked out of the Archbishop's service. He explained the circumstances in another letter to his father:

---

clavier: *a keyboard instrument (from the Latin* clavis, *meaning keys).*

"Well, Count Arco [the Archbishop's chamberlain] has managed things to perfection! – so that is the way to persuade people, to win them over – to refuse petitions out of congenital stupidity, not to say a word to your master for lack of spirit and love of sycophancy, to keep a man hanging about four weeks and at last, when he is obliged to present the petition himself, instead of at least arranging for his admittance, to throw him out and give him a kick in the pants."

Mozart settled in Vienna, determined to make his way in the world without having to work for unsympathetic employers. At first things went well. He took on pupils and his opera *The Abduction from the Seraglio* was a great success. In August 1781 he married Constanze Weber. He had wanted to marry her sister, Aloysia, but she had jilted him two years earlier. In 1787, he was appointed Chamber Composer to Emperor Joseph II. Despite the fact that his salary was less than half that which his predecessor in the post had received, Mozart should have been rich. His operas were popular and he was in demand as a virtuoso pianist. He was constantly in financial trouble, however. Both he and Constanze were hopeless at managing their money. They had to change address eleven times in nine years and much of Mozart's time was taken up in writing begging letters. Many of those he wrote to a fellow Freemason, Michael Puchberg, have survived. Here is one example:

Seraglio: *a sultan's palace or the part of a palace in which his wives were kept.*

Freemason: *member of a secret society founded in London in 1717, pledged to brotherliness and mutual aid. In medieval society, the guild of stonemasons had a system of secret signs and passwords by which they recognized each other.*

"Dearest Brother,

Your true friendship and brotherly love embolden me to ask you for a great favour: I still owe you 8 ducats – and not only am I unable at the moment to repay them, but my confidence in you is so great that I venture to beg you to help me, only until next week (when my concerts at the Casino begin), with the loan of 100 fl. . ."

In 1791, Mozart had his greatest popular success with *The Magic Flute*. Time was already running out for him, however. In the same year, he had been given a commission for a Requiem Mass by a mysterious stranger. There is speculation as to the identity of this patron but it seems likely that he was the agent of a member of the nobility who wished to pass the Requiem off as his own work. Mozart became obsessed with the composition, convinced that it would be his last work. He fell seriously ill but continued to work on the Requiem from his sick-bed. He died before it was completed, the finishing touches being added by his pupil, Sussmayer. The popularity of *The Magic Flute* created a demand for other compositions by Mozart. Very little of his work had been published during his life, but now his wife was able to sell publication rights for a good price. For Mozart, however, commercial success had come too late.

PART TWO

WAR AND REVOLUTION

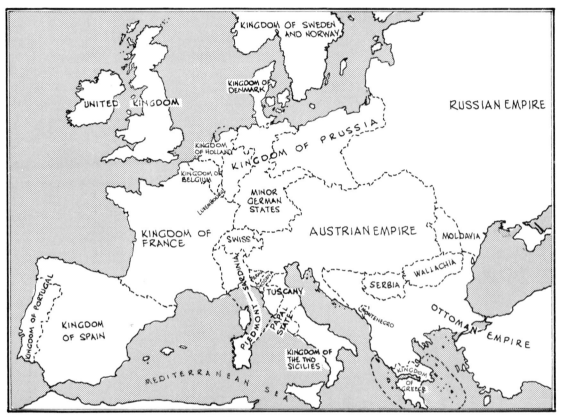

The changes to the map of Europe mentioned in Part One did not come about peacefully. They were the result of a series of wars and revolutions which continued into the present century. The French Revolution of 1798, followed by the conquests of Napoleon, spread new ideas across Europe. The Revolution had shown that there was an alternative to rule by the aristocracy, that ability was more important than noble birth. The slogan of the revolutionaries was *"Liberty, Equality and Brotherhood"*. Nationalism also became a strong force in Europe. Small states which had been swallowed up by one of the larger powers took to arms in

Europe *c.* 1830.

order to gain their independence. In a reversal of this process, Prussia forced the other German states into a united Germany. These national uprisings often developed into full-scale wars as the rival major powers intervened.

The so-called Industrial Revolution, which began in Britain during the eighteenth century (financed by the Slave Trade), also spread eastwards across Europe. The process created a new social class — the industrial workers. Nationalist uprisings were generally led by the middle classes, anxious to gain power at the expense of the aristocracy. The working class in turn fought for their rights, leading to a second wave of uprisings and revolutions. The rapid changes and revolutionary ideas of this period affected all the arts, including music.

The impact of the French Revolution

In 1803, LUDWIG VAN BEETHOVEN began work on his *Eroica* Symphony. It was intended as a tribute to Napoleon Bonaparte, but when Napoleon proclaimed himself Emperor of France, Beethoven scratched out the title page's dedication to "General Bonaparte", exclaiming "so he too is only a mere

On 14 July 1789, an angry crowd stormed and occupied the Bastille, an ancient fortress and prison in Paris. The FRENCH REVOLUTION had begun.

LUDWIG VAN BEETHOVEN. Notice how the ▶ *artist has chosen to picture him in a wild landscape with the storm clouds gathering behind.*

mortal". The symphony, which celebrates the combats, triumphs and death of an idealized hero, was a revolutionary work. Beethoven's first two symphonies had been very much in the tradition of Haydn and Mozart. The *Eroica*, however, broke new ground. For a start, as it lasted for over fifty minutes it was twice as long as an audience would have expected. It was scored for a larger orchestra than was customary, and used more complex harmonies. A review at the time had the following to say: "It lacks nothing, in the way of startling and beautiful passages, in which the energetic and talented composer must be recognized; but it often loses itself in lawlessness."

Beethoven was born in Bonn in 1770, the son of a court musician. His father, recognizing his talent, had hoped to exploit the young Beethoven in the way that Leopold Mozart had done with his son. Beethoven did first come to fame as a pianist in Vienna, but his style was very different from that of Mozart. So powerful was his playing that he had to beg piano manufacturers to make him stronger instruments, as the Viennese pianos of the time could not survive his performances. The main difference between Beethoven and the musicians who had gone before him, however, was that he saw himself as an artist. As far as he was concerned, this made him superior to kings and princes. He was not prepared to be one of the servants in a royal household. His republican ideals did not prevent his accepting royal patronage, but he would not accept anyone as his superior. "It is easy to get on with the nobility if you have something to impress them with."

As an artist, he was careless about his personal surroundings. He was clumsy and had a habit of spitting wherever and whenever the fancy took him. His apartments were dreadfully messy because few servants could put up with his bad temper. One aristocratic visitor described his rooms as "the most disorderly place imaginable" and went on to comment on an unemptied chamber pot which was sitting underneath the piano. Something far more terrible than clumsiness or untidiness was happening to Beethoven, however. As early as 1801, he was complaining about a continual buzzing in his ears. His hearing continued to deteriorate until, by 1817, he was almost completely deaf. Although he had to stop giving piano recitals, Beethoven continued to conduct his music. This was not always successful:

"One could see quite clearly that the poor deaf Master could no longer hear the *piano* passages in his music. But this was particularly obvious at one point in the latter half of the first *Allegro* in the symphony. Here, there are two pauses, in close succession, the second of them being followed by a *pianissimo*. Beethoven must have overlooked the fact, for he began to beat time before the orchestra had even come to the second pause. Thus, without knowing it, he was already ten or twelve bars ahead of the orchestra by the time they resumed playing – *pianissimo* of course."
(From the autobiography of Louis Spohr, 1784-1859)

Despite his deafness, it was during the period from 1818 to his death in 1827 that Beethoven produced his greatest works: the Mass in D (*Missa Solemnis*), the Ninth Symphony and his last five string quartets. The symphony, premiered on 7 May 1824, was a great success despite seemingly impossible odds. There were only two rehearsals and the choir (this was the first symphony to use human voices as well as instruments) and soloists complained that the music was too difficult. Beethoven insisted on conducting himself, but the orchestra followed a second conductor who was standing behind him. At the end Beethoven had to be turned around so that he could see the applause he could not hear.

The last movement of the Ninth Symphony is a musical setting of Schiller's poem "Ode To Joy". Its expressions of joy and universal brotherhood sum up in many ways the impact of the French Revolution upon composers and poets of the early nineteenth century. The bloodshed and violence of the "Reign of Terror" were sufficiently long ago to be forgotten. What survived was a new liberalism in social and

---

piano: *Italian term for "softly" or "quietly" (often abbreviated to* p*).*
pianissimo: *Italian term for "very softly" (often abbreviated to* pp*).*

political thought. a new attitude towards religion, a belief in the importance of the individual and a rise in nationalism. Just as the French Revolution did away with the old order in politics, so a new artistic movement, Romanticism, attempted to replace the old order in the arts.

Romanticism was to be the dominant artistic influence of the nineteenth century. Its main themes were nature and the medieval history of Europe. While the eighteenth century is often known as the "Age of Reason", the Romantics of the nineteenth century preferred to trust to the power of emotion. The period is full of examples of heroic (or just stupid) gestures. In the same year that Beethoven's *Choral* Symphony was first performed, the English poet, Lord Byron, died of fever at Missolonghi in Greece. He had gone there to fight in the Greek war of independence against Turkey. This war appealed to the romantically-minded in Western Europe, who saw it as much more than just a nationalist uprising. In their minds, the realities of nineteenth-century politics and the myths of Ancient Greece had become confused – fatally so in the case of Byron.

There were deliberate attempts to link music with the other arts, especially literature. Romantic composers saw music as a means of self-expression and "programme music" became common, with works depicting different aspects of nature, creating moods or expressing ideals. One of the earliest, and perhaps the best known, of all programme compositions was HECTOR BERLIOZ's *Symphonie Fantastique*. Written in 1830, this symphony, the full title of which was *"Episode de la vie d'un artiste"* (Episode from an Artist's Life), tells of an artist in love. Under the influence of opium, he dreams of the woman with whom he is infatuated. At first, the dreams are pleasant – a ball, a walk in the country – but then they become nightmares. He kills the woman he loves and is condemned to die at the guillotine. Finally, he imagines

The English poet, *GEORGE BYRON (1788-1824).* A great influence on the Romantic movement in the arts, he was also noted for his passionate love affairs. After their first meeting at a ball in 1812, Lady Caroline Lamb described him as *"mad, bad, and dangerous to know"*. He spent much of his life abroad and died in Greece.

himself at a witches' sabbath. The melody which has represented his love throughout the symphony is transformed into a grotesque dance tune. (The possibility of expanding the imagination through the use of drugs was another feature of the Romantic period. Thomas De Quincey had written his *Confessions of an English Opium Eater* in 1821; this was to prove a very influential work.)

Berlioz was inspired to write the *Symphonie Fantastique* by his passion for the Irish actress Harriet Smithson. The poet Heinrich Heine spoke of this infatuation in one of his letters:

HECTOR BERLIOZ (1809-69). His father, a doctor, wanted him to follow a medical career but he was put off after attending his first dissection class. "When I entered that fearful human charnel house, littered with fragments of limbs, and saw the ghastly faces and cloven heads, the bloody cesspool in which we stood, with its reeking atmosphere, the swarms of sparrows fighting for scraps, and the rats in corners, gnawing bleeding vertebrae, such a feeling of horror possessed me that I leaped out of the window and fled home as though Death and all his hideous crew were at my heels . . . and firmly resolved to die rather than enter the career which had been forced on me." (The Lives of the Great Composers)

"My neighbour at that performance [of the *Symphonie Fantastique*] pointed to the composer who sat at the back of the orchestra, beating the timpani, because that's his instrument. "Look at the front box," said my neighbour, "do you see the fat Englishwoman? That's Miss Smithson; Mr Berlioz has been desperately in love with her for three years and we are indebted to that passion for the wild symphony we are getting to hear just now." And there indeed, in the front box, sat the famous Covent Garden actress. Berlioz stared at her all the time, and whenever their eyes met, he hit his drum like a madman. Miss Smithson has become his wife meanwhile and her husband has had a haircut. When I heard his symphony again in the conservatoire last winter, he sat again at the back of the orchestra, handling the timpani, the fat Englishwoman sat in the front box, and their eyes met again — but he did not hit his drums half as furiously. . ."
(*The Lives of the Great Composers*)

Berlioz was the first great composer who was not also a virtuoso instrumentalist. Unable to play any instrument well himself, he developed the modern symphony orchestra as his instrument. He was the first composer to fully exploit its power and range. He dreamed of an orchestra of over four hundred players supported by a choir of more than three hundred voices. A cartoon of the time depicted him conducting an orchestra with a vast array of brass instruments and a percussion section which included cannons. (Fifty years later, Tchaikovsky's *1812 Overture* was to actually call for such a percussion section.) Mozart and Beethoven wrote their piano concertos mainly as a means of displaying their own virtuosity, but the Romantic era saw the beginning of the distinction between composers, conductors and performers.

This was the period of the great virtuoso performers. The greatest of them all was NICCOLÒ PAGANINI, the first musical superstar. He was perhaps the finest violinist who ever lived, but the crowds who flocked to his performances were drawn as much by his image as by the music. He was a tall, dark, very thin Italian, whose brilliant technique was rumoured to be a gift from the Devil. Paganini was a great showman and played up to these rumours. He also used all sorts of tricks to demonstrate his talent. One of his favourites was to deliberately break a string half-way through a performance and continue on only three strings. Paganini was followed by the virtuoso pianists of the nineteenth century, among them FRANZ LISZT. It was Liszt who developed the popular idea of the concert pianist – playing a whole recital from memory, arms raised high, fingers crashing down upon the keys. A famous cartoon shows him raising a whip to a cowering piano. Liszt was the first performer to exploit his good looks. He would stride onto the stage, flick back his shoulder-length hair, and then remove his gloves and throw them to the floor so that women in the audience would fight to get hold of them. Both of these performers fitted the Romantic ideal of the artist as a hero, a concept which can be traced back to Beethoven's *Eroica* Symphony.

The impact of the Industrial Revolution

The Industrial Revolution is the name given to the changes which took place during the eighteenth and nineteenth centuries, first in Britain and gradually across the rest of Europe, and which transformed countries from agricultural to industrial economies. As machines were invented, factories had to be built to house them and coal mined to power them. Houses were built for the factory workers and so industrial towns developed. These grew larger as people left the countryside to find work in the factories. A new wealthy class, the factory owners, challenged the traditional power of the landed aristocracy. This revolution also had its effect upon music.

In the eighteenth century the aristocracy and the Church had been patrons of the arts. Orchestras had been largely private, put together and financed by aristocrats such as Prince Nicholas Esterházy. During the nineteenth century, however, music "went public". The factory owners, anxious to show that they were as cultured as the aristocracy, put money into public buildings, including concert-halls, in the new industrial towns. There had been various forms of public concert, especially opera, since the sixteenth century, but it was during the nineteenth century that the public symphonic concert came into its own. These concerts were very long by modern standards, often with two symphonies and a concerto being

NICCOLÒ PAGANINI (1782-1840). So brilliant was his technique, that many believed he was in league with the devil. The legend of Doctor Faustus, who sold his soul in return for knowledge, was a story which appealed to artists in the Romantic period.

"Chromatic Gallop, executed by the Devil of Harmony." A contemporary cartoon of FRANZ LISZT (1811-86).

performed as well as several shorter works. An increased public awareness of music resulted in transcriptions of a vast number of orchestral works for other instruments, especially the piano.

The nineteenth century was also a period in which musical technology advanced rapidly. Old instruments were modified and new ones were invented. The greatest changes were to wind instruments. The rapid advances in

technology were due to the work of such manufacturers as Böhm and Sax, who between them were responsible for modern wind instruments. Böhm's flute, patented in 1832, opened the way to a modernization of the mechanism of woodwind instruments, which did away with the need for awkward finger positions and eliminated faulty intonation. Even more revolutionary was the introduction of valved trumpets and horns, which enabled them to play all the notes of the chromatic

On 27 September 1825, the world's first passenger railway opened. George Stephenson's "Locomotion" pulled a train the thirty miles from Stockton to Darlington. The coming of the railways revolutionized transport in the nineteenth century.

scale. Although the orchestral brass section tended to be restricted to trumpets, horns, trombones and tuba, several other brass instruments – the cornet, and the tenor and baritone horns – were also developed. The saxophone was invented to combine the advantages of both brass and woodwind instruments. It was never widely used in orchestras, but became an important instrument in military or concert bands. In Britain, the brass

---

intonation: *playing or singing notes "in tune".*

---

chromatic scale: *a thirteen-note scale using consecutive semitones.*

band, using instruments largely developed by Sax, emerged as a working-class alternative to the symphony orchestra. Both concert and brass bands relied extensively upon transcriptions of orchestral music, though in this century they have been seen more and more as musical ensembles in their own right. The composer GUSTAV HOLST, for example, wrote for both forms of band.

Many of the musical ideas of nineteenth-century composers could not have been

The industrial towns which sprang up were dirty and overcrowded. The factories of the nineteenth century created wealth for a few but for those who worked in them, conditions were dreadful. "The workers have nothing to lose but their chains. They have a world to gain. Workers of the world, unite!" (Closing words of The Communist Manifesto *written by Karl Marx and Friedrich Engels in 1848).*

---

concert band: *also known as a military band, contains both brass and woodwind instruments, including saxophones.*

---

brass band: *contains only brass instruments (excluding trumpets and French horns).*

---

realized without this corresponding development in instrument manufacture. An orchestra using the instruments of 1800, for example, would have been incapable of playing the works of Berlioz. Such developments were not confined to orchestral instruments. By the beginning of the nineteenth century, the piano had replaced the harpsichord as the principal keyboard instrument. In 1825, the

During the nineteenth century, the BRASS BAND emerged as a working-class outlet for music. Many factories and mines had their own bands and competition between them was fierce. Such contests have continued into the present century.

invention of the iron frame (in place of wood) increased its power. By 1840, the concert grand had been developed and it reached its modern form by about 1850. Again, it must be remembered that Liszt could never have performed in the way he

1848 was known as "the year of revolutions".
There were uprisings in many parts of Europe.
In Austria, the chancellor, Klemens Metternich,
a strong defender of the absolute power of
kings, was forced to flee. The picture here
shows the Viennese people on the rampage.

did on the kind of piano Mozart or Beethoven were familiar with. He wrote the following note to the manufacturer Pierre Erard:

"My immense success is due, in part, to your magnificent instrument. . . . Now one can no longer say to me that the piano is not a convenient instrument for a large hall, that the sounds are lost there, that the nuances disappear. . . . It is recognised as a fact here that never

has a piano produced a similar effect." (*Larousse Encyclopedia of Music*)

The piano did not just make its mark in the concert-hall. Mass production meant that by the end of the nineteenth century it had become the most popular amateur instrument. It also filled the role of today's record player in many ways. Not everyone could go to concerts, but they could hear, or even learn to play, piano transcriptions of orchestral works.

The impact of nationalism

"I am passionately fond of the national element in all its varied expressions. In a word, I am Russian in the fullest sense of the word."
(Peter Ilyich Tchaikovsky)

Such a statement would have meant little to Bach or Haydn, but during the nineteenth century, people, including composers, began to think of themselves as Russians, Bohemians, Czechs, Italians, Poles or Germans. The old empires were beginning to crumble and the modern nation states of Europe were slowly coming into existence. In Italy and Germany, two opera composers, GIUSEPPE VERDI and RICHARD WAGNER, were closely involved in the struggle for nationhood.

In 1850, Italy was still a collection of separate states ruled by foreign powers, particularly Austria. One state, however, Piedmont-Sardinia, was independent. Its king, Victor Emmanuel, was dedicated to

---

Bohemia: *an independent kingdom from the ninth to the thirteenth century. Part of the Hapsburg Empire until 1918. Now a province of Czechoslovakia.*

achieving Italian unification and independence. Over the next twenty years this aim was realized through a policy of careful involvement in other countries' wars. Verdi, born in 1813, was a passionate nationalist and he was popular for this as much as for his music. His name was scrawled on walls throughout the country and the slogan "*viva Verdi*" was heard everywhere. In fact this was not just a celebration of Verdi's music, popular though it was. The letters V-E-R-D-I also spelt out *Vittorio Emmanuele Ré d'Italia* – Victor Emmanuel, King of Italy. When Italy finally became one nation, Verdi became a deputy in the country's first parliament.

Germany was in a similar position to Italy – a collection of separate states mainly under Austrian domination. Just as Italian unification centred on Piedmont-Sardinia, so German nationalists looked to Prussia. In 1862, Wilhelm I of Prussia appointed Count Otto von Bismarck as his chief minister. Known as "The Iron Chancellor", Bismarck achieved German unification under Prussia in less than ten years. This involved Prussia in wars against Denmark, Austria and France, all deliberately provoked by Bismarck. After the defeat of France, Bismarck had King Wilhelm brought to Paris, where he was declared *Kaiser* (Emperor) of Germany in the Hall of Mirrors at Versailles.

Richard Wagner was born in Leipzig in 1813. In 1842, he was appointed director of the Dresden opera house. In 1848, revolutions broke out in many parts of Europe and Wagner became involved in an insurrection in Dresden. He was forced to flee and began a thirteen-year period of exile, during which he started work on his enormous cycle of operas known as *The Ring*. This vast work consists of four operas – *Das Rheingold (The Rhinegold), Die Valkyrie, Siegfried* and *Gotterdämmerung (The Twilight of the Gods)*. Wagner was obsessed with the history of the German race and was concerned with what he saw as the need to protect German art and culture from alien influence. In later life, these views became more and more extreme. He claimed that the German people, the Aryans, were descended from the gods but had been deprived of their rightful place by inferior peoples, especially the Jews. It is not surprising that Wagner was later to be so popular in Nazi Germany. Adolf Hitler said of him, "Whoever wants to understand National Socialistic Germany must know Wagner".

In 1864, Wagner received a summons from King Ludwig II to come to Bavaria. The eccentric young ruler, popularly known as "Mad King Ludwig", was passionately in love with Wagner's music and probably with Wagner himself. A year later, however, the composer was obliged to go into exile again following a series of scandals, notably his affair with Cosima von Bülow, Liszt's daughter and the wife of the conductor of the Munich Court Opera. Good relations were eventually restored with Ludwig and plans were discussed for the building of a theatre dedicated to the performance of Wagner's works. The result was the opera theatre at Bayreuth, officially opened in 1882. The theatre was revolutionary in its design, with an orchestra pit underneath the stage and room for the hundred or more players demanded by Wagner's vast scores. This orchestra space acts as a sounding box and the singers can actually feel the music beneath their feet. The mixed sound of singers and orchestra is projected out into the enormous fan-shaped amphitheatre.

Valkyrie: *in Norse mythology, the Valkyrie were the women who rode over battlefields to claim the dead heroes chosen by Odin for a place in Valhalla, the great hall in which he dwelt.*

National Socialist: *Nazi.*

Wagner died a year after the theatre opened and it soon became a shrine for lovers of his music.

Nationalism was not confined to Germany and Italy. One of the features of late nineteenth-century classical music was the development of national "schools". Whereas previously composers had turned to Italy or France for inspiration, now they began to explore the cultural traditions of their own countries. This meant listening to folk music, the music of the common people. Artists, particularly in eastern Europe, belonged to a social class which identified more with the conquerors of their country than its peasants, whom they generally despised. Often they did not even speak the same language. FRÉDÉRIC CHOPIN, for example, was a passionate Polish nationalist but he preferred to live in Paris, to where he

The theatre at BAYREUTH, shortly before its opening in 1876. The first Bayreuth season was attended by the Emperor of Germany, the Emperor and Empress of Brazil, the King of Bavaria, Prince George of Prussia, Grand Duke Vladimir of Russia and a host of lesser nobility. Some sixty newspapers from all over the world sent reporters, those from the New York Times *and* Tribune *using the new transatlantic telegraph cable to get their stories through quickly. The correspondent from the London* Times *complained that "the great distance from the town over a dirty road with no shade and no restaurant accommodation caused much discontent".*

moved at the age of twenty-one in 1831. His mazurkas and polonaises, however, derived from Polish folk dances, were a great influence on later nationalist composers. DVOŘÁK and SMETANA in what is now Czechoslovakia, GRIEG in Norway and SIBELIUS in Finland made great use of folk melodies and dance rhythms in their music. In the twentieth century, a more thorough and scientific study of the folk music of Hungary, Romania and Czechoslovakia was carried out by the composers BÉLA BARTÓK and ZOLTÁN KODÁLY.

The idea that a country's character could be expressed through music was most common in Russia. Russian history begins in the sixth century A.D., when towns grew up along the trade routes between Scandinavia and Constantinople (Byzantium). In the ninth century, the Viking *Rus* established their rule over the native *Slavs* and gave their name to the country. Christianity reached Russia in 988 when trading links with Byzantium made it natural to join the Eastern, or Greek Orthodox, branch of the church. Russian culture was thus a mixture of three elements: Slav, Scandinavian and Greek Orthodox. In 1547, the Grand Duke of Moscow, Ivan the Terrible, was crowned as the first Tsar. A later Tsar, Peter the Great (1682-1725), began a process of enforced Westernization, and French became the official language of the court. He built a new capital, St Petersburg, which he called Russia's "window on the West". Russia remained very backward in Western terms, however. The Tsars had absolute rule but, in such a vast country, bureaucrats also had enormous power over the day-to-day life of the population, the majority of whom depended on the land. Serfdom was not abolished until 1861.

Greek Orthodox: *in 330, the Roman Emperor Constantine made the city of Byzantium his capital, renaming it Constantinople. In 395, the Roman Empire was divided into Eastern and Western parts with separate emperors. The Eastern half increasingly adopted the Greek language and way of life. Christianity in the East developed along different lines and in 1054 the Eastern Church split from Rome.*

Until the middle of the nineteenth century, music in Russia was dominated by other European traditions. It was not possible for a native Russian to make an entire career in music. MIKHAIL GLINKA, for instance, the first composer to write an opera on a Russian subject, worked for several years as a civil servant in St Petersburg. There was no tradition of music teaching in Russia, and Russian composers were either self-taught or had studied in other countries. In 1862, this changed, with the foundation of a conservatoire at St Petersburg. The teaching of composition, however, was entrusted to a German called Zaremba who dismissed Glinka and those who shared his ideas as "savages and candle-eaters". Opposed to Zaremba, and dedicated to developing a truly Russian style, was a group of composers known as "The Five". They all had wealthy backgrounds and none was a "trained" musician – the group included a naval officer (RIMSKY-KORSAKOV), a chemist (BORODIN) and an army officer who later became a civil servant (MUSSORGSKY). Their music celebrated the myths and folklore of Russia and the heroes of the country's past. It also used the rhythms of Russian folk music, more complex than those found in the West at the time.

The great enemy of "The Five" was ANTON RUBINSTEIN, founder of the St Petersburg conservatoire and a great champion of Western music. His most famous pupil was Tchaikovsky, whose music contained elements from both sides in this Russian musical feud. Although he used Western forms, the spirit and emotion of his music were totally Russian. After passing his examinations at law school, Tchaikovsky became a civil servant. At the age of twenty-two, however, he became one of the first students at the St

---

conservatoire: *a music school (also called a conservatory).*

An Orthodox church in Kiev. The Rus made *Kiev their capital in the ninth century and it was there that Saint Vladimir, the first Christian ruler of Russia, adopted Christianity in 988. The city remained the Russian capital for three centuries.*

Petersburg conservatoire. He was such a brilliant student that he was soon engaged as a professor at the Moscow conservatoire. He made little money from his compositions, and was resigned to a life of poverty when he met Nadezhda von Meck, a wealthy widow of forty-six. She agreed to pay him a generous allowance on the condition that they never met and kept in touch by letter only. This rather strange relationship gave Tchaikovsky financial independence and he was able to resign from his position at the conservatoire. In the same year that he met his patron, the composer also got married. The marriage was a disaster, and the

couple split up after only nine weeks. Tchaikovsky tried to commit suicide by standing in a river. He was hoping to develop pneumonia, but only managed to catch a cold.

As his music became known throughout Europe, Tchaikovsky travelled more and more, including a visit to the United States in 1891. On his return, he began work on what was to be his last symphony. He said that he had "put his soul" into the work and often "wept bitterly while composing it". Looking for a name for the symphony, Tchaikovsky's brother, Modest, suggested

A group of nineteenth-century Russian ▶ peasants. It was to the traditions of people such as these that the NATIONALIST composers turned. The man in front of the window is playing a balalaika, a traditional Russian instrument. It usually has a triangular body and three strings.

40

first *Tragique* and then *Pathétique*. The latter name was decided upon. Less than a week after conducting the symphony's première in St Petersburg, Tchaikovsky drank a glass of unboiled water and contracted cholera. He died a few days later on 6 November 1893.

Apart from his symphonies, Tchaikovsky is best known for his ballet music. Ballet had become popular in Russia during the reign of Tsar Peter the Great. He imported ballet dancers from Paris and, later, teachers and musicians came to Moscow from Italy and England. In 1860 MARIUS PETIPA, a French dancer and choreographer, was summoned to Russia to create the Russian Imperial Ballet in St Petersburg. Under his direction, it became one of the finest companies in the world and Russian ballet dancers began to earn the reputation in the West that they still hold today. In the early years of the twentieth century, SERGE DIAGHILEV set out to create a truly *Russian* ballet company, as opposed to one dancing in the French tradition. The result was the *Ballet Russe*, made up of young stars from St Petersburg, among them ANNA PAVLOVA and VASLAV NIJINSKY. The *Ballet Russe* took Paris by storm in 1909. Besides the brilliance of the dancing, there was also the music, composed by the then unknown young Russian, IGOR STRAVINSKY. His first three ballet scores, *The Firebird, Petrushka* and *The Rite of Spring*, were an extension of the ideals of "The Five". They drew on the world of Russian folklore and the music and ceremonies of the Russian peasantry. The opening night of *The Rite of Spring* was one of the great scandals in the world of music. The audience was divided into those who supported this exciting new composer and those who did not. Shouting and arguing between these opposing

PETER ILYICH TCHAIKOVSKY (1840-93) aged about thirty.

camps reached such a pitch that the dancers could not hear the orchestra. Nijinsky had to stand in the wings when he was not dancing, beating out the complex rhythms with his feet and hands so that the other dancers could continue.

This violent reaction was not repeated, and Stravinsky's genius was rapidly recognized. He did not return to Russia, however, but remained in Paris where he became part of the cosmopolitan society

◀ *VASLAV NIJINSKY (1892-1950), dancer and choreographer. This photograph was taken in 1914 when he was touring with Diaghilev's* Ballet Russe.

choreographer: *the person who composes the dance steps for a ballet.*

of artists and musicians which made the city the artistic capital of the world at that time. As the century continued, Europe was ravaged by two wars which showed the negative side of nationalism. In 1940, Stravinsky left Paris following the Nazi invasion of France. He spent the rest of his life in the United States, where he died in 1971.

The impact of war

The history of Europe in the eighteenth and nineteenth centuries is one of almost continuous warfare. The majority of these wars were not fought over great matters of principle. Warfare was an instrument of policy, a means of maintaining the status quo or of extending a country's influence. After each war involving the major powers, territories changed hands – an island here, a state there. These wars were fought by relatively small professional armies. Unless fighting actually took place near them, non-combatants were not affected.

The nineteenth-century attitude to war was epitomized by The Charge of the Light Brigade. *In this poem, the terrible military disaster was portrayed as a triumph of British heroism.*

> *"Forward the Light Brigade!*
> *Was there a man dismay'd?*
> *Not tho' the soldier knew*
> *Some one had blunder'd*
> *Their's not to make reply,*
> *Their's not to reason why,*
> *Their's but to do and die:*
> *Into the valley of Death*
> *Rode the six hundred."*

Lord Tennyson was safely at home in England when he wrote those lines, of course. The poets of the First World War, actually involved in the fighting, were to have a very different attitude.

When poets or musicians concerned themselves with warfare, it was to celebrate victories (or, as in the case of the Charge of the Light Brigade, heroic defeats). Handel's oratorio *Judas Maccabaeus*, for example, was composed in 1747 to celebrate the English victory at the Battle of Culloden. There is nothing in this work to suggest the horrific nature of the battle or the appalling treatment meted out to the Scots after their defeat.

Few composers concerned themselves directly with war. Two exceptions were Beethoven and Tchaikovsky, who both wrote compositions concerning the Napoleonic Wars. Beethoven's *Wellington's Victory* was written to celebrate Napoleon's defeat in Spain in 1813. It is not one of his better-known compositions and certainly has none of the power of his other major works, such as the *Eroica* symphony. Tchaikovsky's *1812 Overture* celebrates Napoleon's failure to conquer Russia. It is a strong affirmation of Russian nationalism, but again shows nothing of the reality of warfare.

It was left to the twentieth century to portray this reality. GUSTAV HOLST wrote his *Planets* suite in the summer of 1914. The first movement, "Mars, The Bringer of War", was a prophecy of the total warfare which was to come. Instead of the conventional, comfortable four/four beat of military marches, the movement has a relentless, disturbing five/four rhythm. The brass instruments pursue each other, higher and higher, without ever catching up. The mood is of relentless power and total devastation. More than seventy years later, this piece of music is still one of the most disturbing musical evocations of the horrors of war.

The First World War (1914-18) was Europe's first "total war". It involved almost every country in Europe and armies consisting of conscripted men, not professional soldiers. Civilians, too, were drawn in on a scale not seen before. In addition to all this, the war utilized all the discoveries of the industrial revolution – barbed wire, poison gas, long-range artillery, aeroplanes and tanks. For the first time, members of the university-educated middle classes saw what war was really like. What had for many begun as a great adventure soon became a horrible nightmare. The finest expression of this horror is to be found in the work of the "war poets", among them WILFRED OWEN. Owen was only twenty-five when he was killed in action shortly before the end of the war. His poetry is not about the heroism of war (what he called "the old lie" that it is glorious and fitting to die for one's

THE GREAT WAR shattered for many the idea that war was glorious or heroic. The total number of casualties for both sides, including those wounded or missing was 37,494,186. Over 8 million were killed.

country), but its futility. His poetry is not only about the First World War, but about all war. "My subject is war," he wrote, "and the pity of war." In 1962, BENJAMIN BRITTEN combined some of Owen's poems with the Mass for the Dead in his *War Requiem*. The work was written for the consecration of the new Coventry Cathedral, built to replace the cathedral destroyed during a Second World War bombing raid on the city. Britten dedicated the Requiem to the memory of four friends killed in that war and prefaced the score with Owen's words, "All a poet can do today is warn".

Most music inspired by war is, of course, written far away from the actual scene of the fighting. A notable exception is SHOSTAKOVITCH's seventh symphony, known as *The Leningrad*. In the summer of 1941, the Nazi armies began their attempt to conquer Russia and Leningrad (formerly St Petersburg) was soon under siege. The city was never taken but its inhabitants suffered greatly, and thousands died of starvation. Their struggle took on a symbolic importance, summed up in the following extract from the memorial erected to those who died during the siege.

"Here lie the people of Leningrad
Here the townspeople – the men,
    women and children
Alongside them soldiers – Red Army
    men.
To their last
They defended you, Leningrad,
Cradle of the Revolution . . .

Not forgotten is the hungry, cruel, dark
Winter of 'Forty-One, 'Forty-Two
Nor the ferocity of the bombardments,
Nor the horror of the bombings in 'Forty-
    Three
The whole town smashed.
None of your lives, Comrades, is
    forgotten."

Shostakovitch was a fire-watcher in Leningrad during the siege and he began work on his seventh symphony as the Nazi armies neared the city. It was completed at the end of 1941 and a microfilm of the score, packed in a small tin, was flown to Tehran. From there it went by road to Cairo and by air to the United States. Its first performance was on 19 July 1942 in New York. At the time, it was seen as a purely patriotic work, a tribute to the heroic struggle of the people of Leningrad. Shostakovitch complained that it was often compared to Tchaikovsky's *1812 Overture*. The composer was later to claim a more universal message for the symphony:

"The Seventh Symphony had been
planned before the war and
consequently, it simply cannot be seen
as a reaction to Hitler's attack. The
"invasion theme" has nothing to do with
attack. I was thinking of other enemies
of humanity when I composed the
theme.
    . . . I feel eternal pain for those who
were killed by Hitler, but I feel no less
pain for those who were killed on
Stalin's orders. I suffer for everyone who
was tortured, shot, or starved to death."
(From Simon Volkov (ed), *Testimony –
The Memoirs of Shostakovitch*, Hamish
Hamilton, 1979.)

◀ *The memorial to the victims of the siege of
Leningrad. The siege which lasted from
September 1941 to January 1944, claimed the
lives of 660,000 of the city's inhabitants. 641,803
of these died of hunger.*

PART THREE

BREAKING THE RULES

"Far too many notes."

"The Second Symphony is a filthy monster, a wounded dragon writhing hideously, refusing to die, and in the finale, even though bleeding from every pore, still thrashes about with upraised tail."

"The public was wearied and the musicians puzzled."

"Simply noise . . . an impression of grim violence and dreary vagueness."

"Could we ever learn to love such music?"

At first sight these could be the comments of traditionally-minded music lovers, outraged by some discordant modern composition. In fact, that is what they are, except that they are contemporary complaints about compositions by, in order, Mozart, Beethoven, Brahms, Wagner and Tchaikovsky. "Breaking rules", pushing forward the limits of what is acceptable in music, is not a habit peculiar to twentieth-century composers. What is different in this century, however, is the pace of change. Improved transport and communication and modern recording techniques mean that new ideas can spread much more quickly – and can also become outdated more quickly. These same technological improvements, however, also mean that we have access to music from earlier periods. When Bach took up his post as cantor at Leipzig, he threw away all of his predecessor's music and fully expected the same to be done with his. The twentieth century, though a period of such rapid change, is also a time

when much effort is made to preserve and learn from the past.

Romanticism dominated the music of the nineteenth century, but by the end of the century a reaction against it had already begun, particularly in France. ERIK SATIE (1866-1925) was strongly opposed to what he saw as the excesses of Wagner and other German composers. His own compositions were very economical and often given humorous titles – *Piece in the Form of a Pear*, for example. He gave up his studies at the Paris Conservatoire to work as a café pianist and many of his works show the influence of ragtime. He was also one of the first composers to use non-musical sounds in his compositions. His ballet music, *Parade*, includes the sound of a ship's foghorn and clattering typewriters. He remained comparatively unknown, but had a great influence on other French composers, such as CLAUDE DEBUSSY.

Debussy was born in 1862 and entered the Paris Conservatoire as a student of piano at the age of ten. Two important

The Gramophone and Typewriter Company ▶ *(later to become HMV) was founded in 1898. Its early recordings were of singers, such as the Italian tenor, Enrico Caruso (1873-1921). It was not until the development of electrical recording in the 1920s that it became possible to record orchestral works. The invention of the long-playing disc in 1950 meant that longer works, such as symphonies, no longer had to be spread over several records. Modern studio techniques mean that recordings can be edited to produce a "perfect" performance. The photographs show an early example of a horn gramophone and a control room at EMI's Abbey Road studios in London in 1987.*

influences on his musical career were a performance of Indonesian *gamelan* music that he heard at the Paris International Exhibition of 1889 and his meeting with Satie. In 1905 he composed *La Mer*, a musical evocation of the sea, which led to his music being linked with the paintings of Impressionists such as MONET and RENOIR. Where the Impressionist painters attempted to capture experiences through the shifting effects of natural light, Debussy used shimmering patterns of musical timbre.

Just as the French Revolution was to have a lasting impact upon the music of the nineteenth century, so the First World War was to have a profound effect on that of the twentieth. In particular, the reaction against the idealism of Romanticism was given a new impetus. This reaction displayed itself in several ways.

First, there was a movement known as "Neo-Classicism", a conscious return to the forms of the eighteenth century, represented in a modern way. Other composers, notably a group in Paris known as "The Six", deliberately used elements from the music-hall and jazz. After the chaos of the war, there was also an effort to find a totally ordered, almost mathematical form of music. ARNOLD SCHOENBERG (1874-1951) devised a system of harmony in which all twelve notes of the Western chromatic scale are given equal worth – in other words, there is no idea of a piece of music being in a particular key. These notes are then arranged by the composer in a sequence with each note appearing only once. This is the "tone row" from which the rest of the composition is built. It can be inverted or played backwards, but it still governs the whole piece. This kind of formal approach was also applied to such elements as note duration, timbre and pitch by the French composer OLIVIER MESSIAEN. The term "serial music" was used to describe such compositions. Later, this technique was modified and composers such as STOCKHAUSEN began to introduce elements of chance into their music. The American, JOHN CAGE, took this to an extreme, deciding upon notes by the throw of a dice. During the 1940s, musicians also began to experiment with electronic methods of sound production.

These experiments, exciting though they were to musicians, did not always meet with the approval of a public more at home with nineteenth-century music. On a more serious level, during the 1930s they also met with government disapproval in Germany and the Soviet Union. In Germany, Hitler exploited the German sense of failure after the First World War, claiming that the country had not been defeated militarily but had been betrayed by "undesirables" ("stabbed in the back"). When the Nazi party came to power, the purging of these "undesirables" – particularly Jews and Communists – began. There was also an attempt to stamp out what was referred to as

---

ragtime: *a style of piano music developed in the United States in the late nineteenth century. It combines a regular bass line with syncopated melodies.*

---

gamelan: *an Indonesian percussion orchestra made up largely of instruments of the xylophone family.*

---

timbre: *the particular tone colour of an instrument.*

CLAUDE ACHILLE DEBUSSY (1862-1918), most ▶ famous of the French "Impressionist" composers. He was influenced by the music of ERIK SATIE. "I explained to Debussy," wrote Satie, "that I was in no way anti-Wagnerian but that we should have a music of our own – if possible, without any sauerkraut. Why could we not use the means that Claude Monet, Cézanne, Toulouse-Lautrec and others had made known? Why could we not transpose those means to music?"

"degenerate" art. PAUL HINDEMITH (1895-1963), teacher of composition at the Musikhochschule in Berlin, openly objected to the nationalistic doctrines of Hitler and his minister of propaganda, Goebbels. Branded as a defender of "degenerate, effete, anti-German art", he was forced to flee the country. Schoenberg also left Germany when the Nazis came to power, and finally settled in the United States. Although he was born a Jew, he had converted to Roman Catholicism, but in 1933 he reverted to his Jewish faith as a sign of solidarity with the

ADOLF HITLER at a Nazi rally in 1934. There was no room for artistic experiment in Hitler's Germany.

answer a challenge given in English.

Following the 1917 Revolution, artists in Russia enjoyed a period of great freedom, and experimentation was officially encouraged. During the 1930s, however, this policy changed. Lenin's statement that "Art belongs to the people" was interpreted by his successor, Stalin, to mean that artists should serve, and be controlled by, the state. Whereas Hitler linked *avant garde* music with Communism, Stalin branded it as a tool of the Western enemies of the Soviet Union. The concept of "Socialist Realism" was born, with all art turned into propaganda. Stravinsky's music was condemned as the "reactionary essence of modernism as an anti-folk end in art, reflecting the decadent ideology of the imperialist bourgeoisie". The worst crime a composer could be accused of was "*formalism*". The composer PROKOFIEV, himself a victim of official displeasure, described formalism as "the name given to music not understood on its first hearing".

The absolute power wielded by Stalin is illustrated in a story told by Shostakovitch in his memoirs. One night Stalin phoned the Radio Committee to ask if they had a record of Maria Yudina playing Mozart's Piano Concerto no. 23. The terrified recipient of the call said they had, though in fact no such record existed. Stalin asked for it to be brought to him the next day. The

victims of Hitler's persecution. Schoenberg's pupil, ANTON WEBERN, remained in Nazi-occupied Austria throughout the war, despite official condemnation of his music. Ironically, in the closing stages of the war he was killed by an American soldier when he failed to

Lenin: *Vladimir Ilyich Ulyanov (1870-1924). Leader of the 1917 Russian Revolution.*

Stalin: *Josef Vissarionovich Djugashvili (1879-1953). Became Russian leader after the death of Lenin. He crushed all opposition, particularly in the great purges of 1934-37, and established the USSR as a world power.*

54

panic-stricken committee called in Yudina and an orchestra and recorded that night. Shostakovitch continues:

> "Yudina later told me that they had to send the conductor home, he was so scared he couldn't think. They called another conductor, who trembled and got everything mixed up, confusing the orchestra. Only a third conductor was in any shape to finish the recording. I think this is a unique event in the history of recording – I mean, changing conductors three times in one night. Anyway, the record was ready by morning. They made one single copy in record time and sent it to Stalin."

Shostakovitch was constantly in trouble with the authorities, but he survived because even Stalin recognized him as the Soviet Union's greatest living composer. In 1948, a resolution of the Central Committee of the Communist Party listed several composers, including Shostakovitch, Prokofiev and Khachaturian, as artists "in whose work formalist perversions and anti-democratic tendencies in music, alien to the Soviet people and its artistic tastes, were particularly glaring". The composers had to apologize publicly for their "crimes". Shostakovitch expressed gratitude for "all the criticism contained in the resolution", promising to work "with still more determination . . . on the musical depiction of the images of the heroic Soviet people". In 1953, Stalin died and Shostakovitch began work on his Tenth Symphony, a work which, in the composer's own words, was "about Stalin and the Stalin years". The Scherzo is a musical portrait of the dictator, while in the slow movement a melody in the strings twists and turns, constantly beaten down by hammer blows from the brass. Although there was a more liberal atmosphere in Russia after Stalin's death, Shostakovitch still could not make the theme of the symphony public. It was only in his memoirs, published after his own death in 1975, that he could speak freely. His funeral was attended by many of those who had denounced him in earlier years and the obituary, published in the official Soviet press, described him as "the great composer of our times. . . . A faithful son of the Communist Party, an eminent social and government figure, citizen-artist D.D. Shostakovitch".

Stalin and Hitler were not the only leaders to recognize the power of music. The Hungarian ZOLTÁN KODÁLY, whose works were often inspired by folk music, became involved in his country's uprising against the Soviet Union in 1956. The Greek composers MIKIS THEODORAKIS and YANNIS XENAKIS found themselves in trouble with the military regime which ruled their country in the late 1960s and early 1970s. Political interference with music is not unique to the twentieth century. The Italian censors forced Verdi to change the location of his opera *Un Ballo in Maschera* from Sweden to America in order to avoid offending the Swedish government. Even Mozart earned official displeasure with *Le Nozze di Figaro*, because the opera's story – the fooling of an aristocrat by a pair of common people – was revolutionary for its day. Popular and folk music have also come under attack in many countries with authoritarian governments – Chile and Greece, for example. In South Africa it is against the law to listen to the music of MIRIAM MAKEBA.

Shostakovitch's Fifth Symphony was composed in 1937, at the height of Stalin's purges. The première was in Leningrad, where there had been particularly harsh repression, and many members of the audience wept openly. The Russian author

---

Un Ballo in Maschera: *"A Masked Ball".*

Ilya Ehrenburg made the following comment about it, a judgement which can be applied to all great music: "Music has a great advantage: without mentioning anything, it can say everything."

MOZART'S REQUIEM is performed in 1980 in Gdansk, Poland, to commemorate the deaths ten years earlier of shipyard workers on strike.

THE SYMPHONY ORCHESTRA

The modern symphony orchestra consists of seventy or more musicians. Instruments are divided into four sections: strings, woodwind, brass and percussion. A chamber orchestra is much smaller, often containing only strings but occasionally adding wind players. It must be remembered that orchestras in the eighteenth and early nineteenth centuries were much smaller. Most instruments were developed gradually through a process of trial and error. The following list shows when they made their first orchestral appearance in their modern form.

Strings
From the fifteenth to the seventeenth

The LONDON SYMPHONY ORCHESTRA in the Barbican Hall, London.

century, the most popular stringed instrument was the viol. This differed from the violin in that it had a flat rather than an arched back, a fretted finger board (like a guitar) and "c" rather than "f" shaped sound-holes. There were four members of the family: treble, alto, tenor and bass. All had six strings and were played resting either on or between the legs.

The modern stringed instruments, violin, viola, violoncello and double bass, were developed from the viol in northern Italy during the sixteenth century. They made their first orchestral appearance in about 1600. The harp, an ancient instrument, reached its modern form by the end of the eighteenth century.

Woodwind

The modern Böhm flute dates from 1832, though Lully used a flute in his orchestra as early as 1672. The recorder was also used in seventeenth-century orchestras.

The name "piccolo" dates from 1856, but small "octave flutes" were in use from the early eighteenth century.

The oboe originated in the Middle Ages. Its name comes from the French word *hautbois*, meaning "loud wood". Its first orchestral use was by Lully in 1657.

The cor anglais, or "tenor oboe", was introduced in 1760.

The clarinet was developed by J.C. Denner (1655-1707) who modified and improved a single-reed folk instrument, the chalumeau. The lower register of the clarinet is still referred to as the *chalumeau* register, while the upper register is called the *clarion*, after the high trumpet parts known as *clarino*. The first orchestral use of the clarinet was in 1726.

The bass clarinet joined the woodwind section in 1838.

The bassoon was developed from an earlier double-reed bass instrument called the curtal. In the seventeenth century it was used in orchestras as a bass oboe. The double bassoon has a range an octave lower.

Adolphe Sax invented the saxophone in 1840. It has had a limited orchestral use.

Brass

The natural trumpet (no valves) dates back to prehistoric times. Such an instrument is only capable of producing the notes of the harmonic series. These harmonics are related by mathematical ratios to give a series of decreasing intervals. From the first harmonic, or fundamental, to the second is an octave. From the second to the third is a fifth, from the third to the fourth is a fourth, followed by a third and so on. Far more notes can be produced in the upper register, which is why trumpet parts in Bach's music, for example, are always so high. The introduction of valves in the early nineteenth century enabled the player to divert the passage of air through additional lengths of tubing, thus producing different sets of harmonics. Earlier attempts at increasing the chromatic range of the trumpet had included a slide mechanism (like a trombone's) and a keyed instrument (for which Haydn wrote his trumpet concerto).

The first valved brass instrument was the horn, fitted with a mechanism for which a patent was taken out by Friedrich Blühmel in 1818. Before that, horn players had used the position of their hand inside the bell to alter the pitch of a note, and so increase the number of different notes they could play. Such "natural horns" were used in orchestras from the early seventeenth century.

The trombone was developed from the Roman slide-trumpet by way of the medieval sackbut. It achieved its modern form in about 1500 and was used in orchestras from about 1600 as part of the bass line. In 1870, a valve trombone was introduced but it did not replace the slide instrument.

The first modern tuba was developed in Berlin in 1835. An earlier keyed instrument, the ophicleide, had been developed in France in 1817.

Other members of the brass family were developed during the nineteenth century but, apart from the cornet, none were used in orchestras. For a while, particularly in France, the cornet threatened to replace the trumpet.

Percussion

The timpani ("kettle drums") originated in the Orient and were first used in orchestras in about 1600.

Cymbals came from Turkey, and joined the orchestra in 1680.

The bass drum and side drum were added in the eighteenth century.

The triangle, gong and glockenspiel had their first orchestral use at about the same time.

The xylophone and tambourine were not added until a century later.

During the twentieth century, composers have used an ever-increasing number of percussion instruments, including many from Latin America.

HISTORICAL PERIODS

For the sake of convenience, musicians are divided into historical periods. Obviously, these are not absolute divisions – some composers overlap periods – but they do provide a useful guide.

Baroque: 1600-1750
Gabrielli, Giovanni (1557-1612)
Monteverdi, Claudio (1567-1633)
Lully, Jean Baptiste (1632-87)
Purcell, Henry (1658-95)
Telemann, Georg Phillip (1681-1767)
Bach, Johann Sebastian (1685-1750)
Handel, George Frideric (1685-1759)

Classical: 1750-1800
Bach, Carl Philip Emanuel (1714-88)
Haydn, Franz Joseph (1732-1809)
Mozart, Wolfgang Amadeus (1756-91)

Romantic: 1800-50
Beethoven, Ludwig van (1770-1827)
Paganini, Niccolò (1782-1840)
Rossini, Gioacchino (1792-1868)
Schubert, Franz (1797-1828)
Berlioz, Hector (1803-69)
Mendelssohn, Felix (1809-47)
Chopin, Frédéric François (1810-49)
Schumann, Robert (1810-56)
Liszt, Franz (1811-86)

Wagner, Richard (1813-83)
Verdi, Giuseppe (1813-1901)
Smetana, Bedrich (1824-84)
Brahms, Johannes (1833-97)
Tchaikovsky, Peter Ilyich (1840-93)
Dvořák, Antonin (1841-1904)
Grieg, Edvard Hagerup (1843-1907)

Modern: 1900 onwards
Debussy, Claude (1862-1918)
Strauss, Richard (1864-1949)
Sibelius, Jean (1865-1957)
Satie, Erik (1866-1925)
Schoenberg, Arnold (1874-1951)
Ives, Charles (1874-1951)
Ravel, Maurice (1875-1937)
Bartók, Béla (1881-1945)
Stravinsky, Igor (1882-1971)
Webern, Anton (1883-1945)
Hindemith, Paul (1897-1963)
Shostakovitch, Dmitri (1906-75)
Britten, Benjamin (1913-1977)

Avant-garde: experimental modern music
Cage, John (b. 1912)
Xenakis, Iannis (b. 1922)
Ligeti, Gyorgy (b. 1923)
Stockhausen, Karlheinz (b. 1928)

THE MUSIC

Other books in this series have included a discography. In the case of classical music, there is such an enormous number of records that this would be impossible. Instead, here is a list of some of the most popular compositions of some of the composers mentioned in the preceding pages. All are readily available and most public libraries now have a large selection of classical music records which you can borrow. This list should be used only as a starting point: there is a world of music waiting to be explored and the real enjoyment is in finding your own favourites.

Bach, Johann Sebastian
Brandenburg Concertos

Handel
Suite *Water Music*
Suite *Music for the Royal Fireworks*

Haydn
"Surprise" Symphony

Mozart
"Eine Kleine Nachtmusik"

Beethoven
Symphony No. 9 "The Choral" – last movement

Berlioz
"Symphonie Fantastique" – fourth movement

Wagner
"Ride of the Valkyrie"
Lohengrin – prelude to Act Two.

Verdi
Aïda – finale, Act II

Smetana
Vltava

Tchaikovsky
Swan Lake – ballet music

Dvořák
Symphony No. 5 "From the New World" – second movement

Grieg
Peer Gynt – incidental music

Satie
"Trois Gymnopédies" – written for piano, but also arranged for orchestra by Debussy

Debussy
La Mer

Ravel
Bolero
Pictures from an Exhibition – an orchestration of music originally written for the piano by Mussorgsky

Stravinsky
The Rite of Spring

Holst
Suite *The Planets*

Shostakovitch
Symphony No. 7 "The Leningrad" – first movement

Bartók
"Concerto for Orchestra"

MAP

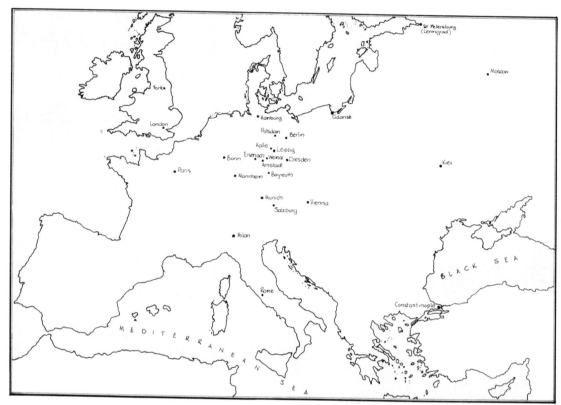

Places in Europe mentioned in the text.

DATE LIST

1517 – Martin Luther condemned for heresy.
   – Start of the Reformation
1534 – Ignatius Loyola forms the "Company of Jesus" (Jesuits)
1560 – Religious wars in France.
   – Thirty years of civil war.
1618 – Start of the "Thirty Years War" in central Europe
1642 – Civil war in England (ends 1651)
1652 – Series of wars between Britain and Holland (ends 1674)
1675 – Prussia defeats Sweden in battle.
   – Rise of Prussian military power
1683 – Turks defeated outside Vienna
1696 – Peter the Great begins westernization of Russia
1701 – Britain and Austria at war with France (ends 1713)
1739 – War between Britain and Spain
1740 – Britain and Austria at war with France (ends 1748)
1746 – Scots defeated by English at Battle of Culloden
1956 – Britain and Prussia at war with France and Austria (ends 1763)
1776 – American Declaration of Independence
1789 – French Revolution begins
1796 – French, under Napoleon, at war with other European powers
1804 – Napoleon becomes Emperor of France
1815 – Final defeat of Napoleon at Waterloo (in Belgium)

1829 – Greece wins independence from Turkey
1830 – Belgium gains independence from Holland
1848 – Revolutions and uprisings in many parts of Europe
   – Communist Manifesto produced by Karl Marx and Freidrich Engels
1854 – Crimean War. Britain and France against Russia (ends 1855)
1861 – Victor Emmanuel declared king of united Italy
1866 – Prussia defeats Austria
1870 – Prussia defeats France
1871 – Wilhelm I of Prussia declared Emperor of Germany
1876 – War between Serbia and Turkey
1877 – Russia enters war on Serbian side. Turkey defeated
1897 – Greece and Turkey at war
1905 – Norway gains independence from Sweden
1914 – Outbreak of First World War
1917 – Russian Revolution
1918 – End of First World War
1921 – Irish Free State set up
1933 – Adolf Hitler appointed Chancellor of Germany
1936 – Civil war in Spain
1939 – Germany invades Poland. Start of Second World War
1945 – End of Second World War

INDEX